PLANET UNDER PRESSURE
ANIMALS UNDER THREAT

Louise and Richard Spilsbury

www.raintreepublishers.co.uk

Visit our website to find out more information about **Raintree** books.

To order:
- ☎ Phone 44 (0) 1865 888112
- 🗎 Send a fax to 44 (0) 1865 314091
- 💻 Visit the Raintree bookshop at **www.raintreepublishers.co.uk** to browse our catalogue and order online.

Produced for Raintree by
Monkey Puzzle Media Ltd
Gissing's Farm, Fressingfield
Suffolk IP21 5SH, UK

First published in Great Britain by Raintree,
Halley Court, Jordan Hill, Oxford OX2 8EJ,
part of Harcourt Education.
Raintree is a registered trademark
of Harcourt Education Ltd.

Editorial: Clare Weaver
Design: Jane Hawkins
Picture Research: Laura Barwick
Production: Chloe Bloom

Originated by Dot Gradations
Printed and bound in China by South China
Printing Company

10 digit ISBN 1 4062 0537 0
13 digit ISBN 978 1 4062 0537 4
11 10 09 08 07
10 9 8 7 6 5 4 3 2 1

**British Library Cataloguing in
Publication Data**
Spilsbury, Richard, 1963–
Animals under threat. – (Planet under pressure)
1.Wildlife conservation – Juvenile literature
2.Endangered species – Juvenile literature
3.Animal ecology – Juvenile literature
I,Title II.Spilsbury, Louise
333.9'542

Acknowledgements
Corbis pp. **13** (Juda Ngwenya/Reuters), **15** (Perry
Conway), **30** (Sergeo Karpukhin/Reuters); Durrell
Wildlife Conservation Trust p. **37**; FLPA pp. **10
right** (Frans Lanting/Minden Pictures), **22** (Tui

Cover photograph of tiger cubs reproduced with
permission of Still Pictures (Schafer & Hill) and of
poached elephant ivory with permission of Getty
Images (Tom Stoddart Archive).

Every effort has been made to contact copyright
holders of any material reproduced in this book.
Any omissions will be rectified in subsequent
printings if notice is given to the publishers.

Disclaimer
All the Internet addresses (URLs) given in this
book were valid at the time of going to press.
However, due to the dynamic nature of the
Internet, some addresses may have changed, or
sites may have changed or ceased to exist since
publication. While the author and publishers
regret any inconvenience this may cause readers,
no responsibility for any such changes can be
accepted by either the author or the publishers.

T

7

3

-

2

Contents

Any words appearing in the text in bold,
like this, are explained in the Glossary.

Animal biodiversity around the world

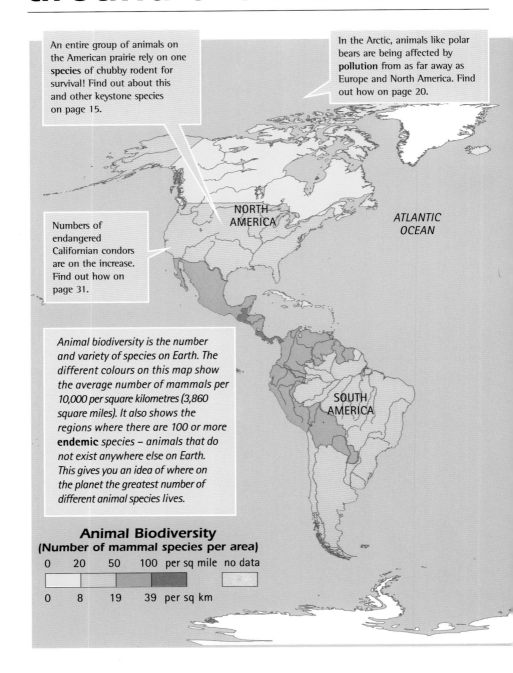

An entire group of animals on the American prairie rely on one **species** of chubby rodent for survival! Find out about this and other keystone species on page 15.

In the Arctic, animals like polar bears are being affected by **pollution** from as far away as Europe and North America. Find out how on page 20.

Numbers of endangered Californian condors are on the increase. Find out how on page 31.

*Animal biodiversity is the number and variety of species on Earth. The different colours on this map show the average number of mammals per 10,000 per square kilometres (3,860 square miles). It also shows the regions where there are 100 or more **endemic** species – animals that do not exist anywhere else on Earth. This gives you an idea of where on the planet the greatest number of different animal species lives.*

NORTH AMERICA

ATLANTIC OCEAN

SOUTH AMERICA

Animal Biodiversity
(Number of mammal species per area)

| 0 | 20 | 50 | 100 | per sq mile | no data |

| 0 | 8 | 19 | 39 | per sq km |

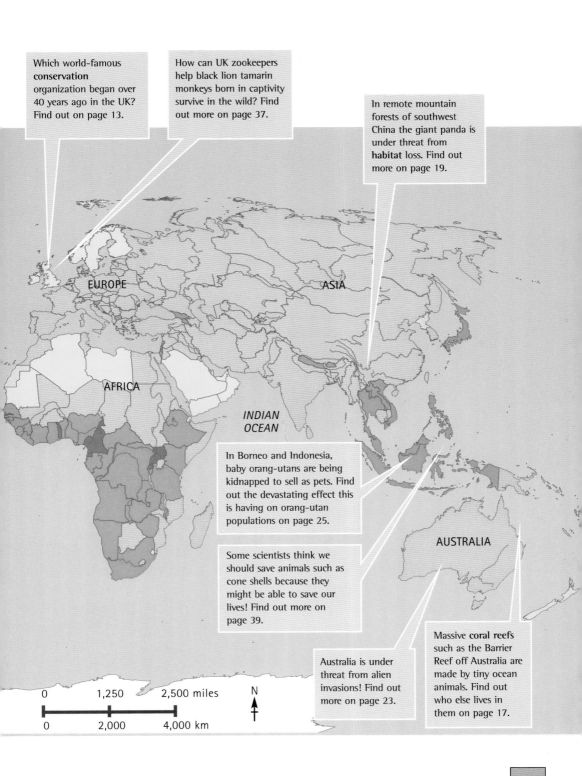

Which world-famous **conservation** organization began over 40 years ago in the UK? Find out on page 13.

How can UK zookeepers help black lion tamarin monkeys born in captivity survive in the wild? Find out more on page 37.

In remote mountain forests of southwest China the giant panda is under threat from **habitat** loss. Find out more on page 19.

EUROPE

ASIA

AFRICA

INDIAN OCEAN

In Borneo and Indonesia, baby orang-utans are being kidnapped to sell as pets. Find out the devastating effect this is having on orang-utan populations on page 25.

AUSTRALIA

Some scientists think we should save animals such as cone shells because they might be able to save our lives! Find out more on page 39.

Massive **coral reefs** such as the Barrier Reef off Australia are made by tiny ocean animals. Find out who else lives in them on page 17.

Australia is under threat from alien invasions! Find out more on page 23.

0   1,250   2,500 miles

N

0   2,000   4,000 km

The world's animals

Humans are just one of the two million **species** of animals identified by scientists on our planet. But many experts believe that there could be 10 million or more species yet to be discovered and identified on Earth. Many of these are small creatures, such as insects, or organisms that live in as yet unexplored depths of the oceans or dark rainforests.

EXTINCTION IN THE PAST

It is normal and natural for some species to die out gradually and become **extinct** over time. There have also been five mass extinctions since Earth formed, when 50 per cent or more of all species became extinct in a relatively short period of time. In the past, these mass extinctions were caused by natural phenomena, such as volcanic eruptions or sudden **climate change**. For example, many scientists believe dinosaurs became extinct 65 million years ago when Earth's climate was transformed by an enormous meteorite impact.

Animals live in every different habitat on Earth. These emperor penguins spend their entire lives in the Antarctic, where sub-zero temperatures would kill many other species.

As European settlers spread across North America in the early 19th century they hunted the bison almost to extinction. Bison numbers dropped from 60–100 million to just 750 by 1890. Since 1900, numbers have increased and today there are around 350,000.

EXTINCTION RATES TODAY

The usual rate of natural, gradual extinction is something like one species per million species a year. However, today, species are disappearing around 1,000 times faster than this. In the last 500 years, 850 known species have died out, and up to 16,000 others are under threat. Unless the present trend is reversed, some scientists predict that the world could lose about 55 per cent of its species over the next 50 to 100 years, creating a sixth mass extinction.

ANIMALS UNDER THREAT

Many animals today are becoming extinct as a result of human activities, such as hunting, **habitat** destruction, or **pollution**, and not because of natural changes. Each day, the world's human population grows by 200,000 people and we have a greater and greater impact on the world's environments and wildlife. Even though people are trying to improve the situation through **conservation** – protecting or conserving the world's animals and habitats – species numbers are still decreasing. Many people believe that the decline in animal species is one of the greatest threats facing Earth today.

Where do the world's animals live?

Animals can be found all over Earth, from the coldest mountaintops to the hottest deserts. These different areas are called **biomes**. A biome is a large geographical area with distinctive plant and animal groups that are adapted to its particular habitats – for example, a rainforest or desert. All Earth's habitats vary in altitude (height), temperature, moisture, light, soil, and many other factors.

HABITAT AND CLIMATE

Differences in **climate** have a huge effect on animal life in any area. Desert biomes form in areas with a very hot, dry climate. Desert animals have features that enable them to survive the heat and lack of rain. For example, camels can survive without water for days, and have thick fur to protect them from burning sun. Many animals living in freezing climates, such as the **tundra**, have lots of body fat, for insulation against the cold and some, such as polar bears and Arctic hares, have white hair to camouflage them against the snow.

Reindeer, or caribou, have stomachs adapted to feed on the lichen that grows in the tundra and they have two layers of fur to keep them warm.

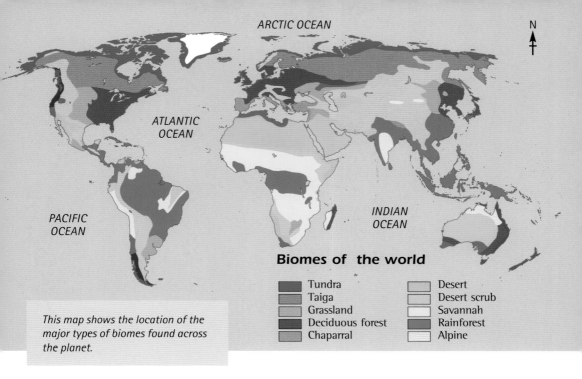

This map shows the location of the major types of biomes found across the planet.

DIVERSITY AND GEOGRAPHY

Some biomes of the world have a greater number of different species than others. Not surprisingly, the dry, freezing, and treeless tundra has the lowest number of species or **species diversity**. For instance, here there are only a few hundred species of insect. Whereas tropical biomes, such as rainforests, where it is warm and wet all year round and there are a variety of different habitats, have the highest number of different species. There are over one million insect species in rainforests. Rainforests cover only 7 per cent of the planet but contain over half of all known species on Earth.

BIODIVERSITY HOTSPOTS

Conservation International, an international conservation organization, has identified 25 **biodiversity** "hotspots". Biodiversity means the number and variety of species in an area. Biodiversity hotspots are regions, such as the Upper Amazon, New Zealand, and Hawaii, which contain a wealth of different species in a relatively small area. Each hotspot faces extreme threats. In some regions this is because human populations are growing so fast that people are spreading into wild areas. More than 1.1 billion people live in the 25 biodiversity hotspots and population growth in these areas is more than double the world average. In other hotspots, it is their resources, such as trees or fertile soil, which are in great demand.

On their isolated island home, free from competition with the monkeys that drove African lemurs to extinction, the lemurs of Madagascar evolved into around 50 different and unique species.

Animal biodiversity

The range and variety of animal species on our planet is amazing. What is even more amazing is that scientists believe that they are all descendants of a single, simple group of organisms that lived millions of years ago.

WHAT IS EVOLUTION?

Every individual animal is slightly different, making it more or less able than others to survive in a particular climate or situation. Individuals who are better suited or **adapted** are more likely to survive and reproduce, while other animals die out. The young of the successful animals will inherit some of these advantageous characteristics. Over many generations, these changes can result in completely new species developing from a single original species. This is called **evolution**.

IN THE PAST

The evolution of different species also happens when a population of animals is separated. For example, 200 million years ago Earth's continents were joined together as a giant landmass called Pangaea. This gradually split into smaller pieces, which drifted to new positions on the planet and new kinds of habitats formed. Groups of animals that once all lived together on the same land were separated and had to adapt to new local habitats. Over time, the separated populations became different to each other – so different that they could no longer breed with each other – and they became separate species.

The Galapagos cormorant evolved on islands where it had no predators. Without the need to fly, it gradually evolved into a flightless bird.

ISLAND LIFE

Looking at animal species on islands can help us understand how evolution works. Many islands are home to **endemic** species, which means the species there are found only in that region and do not exist elsewhere. They developed from their ancestors in geographical isolation, with little competition from other animals for food or space. Charles Darwin made many of his discoveries about evolution on the Galapagos Islands, South America, in the 19th century. The endemic species here include giant tortoises, flightless cormorants, and marine iguanas.

HOW DOES CLASSIFICATION WORK?

Classification is the grouping of different species of living things. It helps us to understand the differences and similarities between different organisms. The different animal species are classified using a system devised by Swedish scientist Carl Linne in the mid-18th century. Using the Linnaean system, each species has a two-part scientific name. These names are written in Latin and are recognized worldwide. Each year 15,000 new species are classified.

Animals in danger

There are thousands of scientists at work around the world examining populations of different species of animals. The International Union for the Conservation of Nature and Natural Resources (IUCN) uses this data to compile the IUCN Red List of Threatened Species. This is a global directory of the levels of threat faced by different species.

LEVELS OF THREAT

The Red List highlights four main categories of threatened animals, depending on how high a risk of extinction they face. Critically endangered species, such as the black rhino, face an extremely high risk of extinction in the wild. Endangered animals, such as orang-utans, face a very high risk of extinction in the near future. Vulnerable species, such as the wandering albatross, are at high risk of extinction. Species of animal, such as the bull shark, are defined as lower risk. They need conservation measures to ensure they do not become endangered.

In the 1970s, the American alligator, found along the coasts of southeast United States, was an endangered species. Today, thanks to stricter hunting laws and more conservation officers, it is now in the "lower risk" category of the IUCN Red List.

World Wildlife Fund

The World Wildlife Fund (WWF) is one of the largest conservation organizations in the world. It was set up in 1961 by a group of wildlife enthusiasts, who were shocked by the destruction of habitats and wildlife in Africa and elsewhere.

They realised that much of the world's wildlife was in danger of being wiped out. Today, WWF runs around 1,300 conservation projects at any one time. It has nearly five million supporters and works in more than 100 countries around the globe.

One of WWF's many projects is releasing black rhinos back into protected areas of land in South Africa.

CONSERVATION

One reason for defining threats to wildlife is to find out which animals need most help and why. Individuals and organizations across the world are working to save endangered animals and their habitats. Some conservationists work on protecting habitats, for example, by creating **reserves,** while others exert pressure on governments to create laws to protect animals, such as making it illegal to hunt particular species.

WHAT DO YOU THINK?
Conservation only for flagship species?

- Conservation campaigns often highlight **flagship species** – large, appealing animals, such as tigers, pandas, and whales – to get public support.
- Saving them involves protecting their habitat, which also protects all species in it, but does this encourage us to care only about "attractive" species?

All living things have basic needs and depend on other living things to meet those needs. When bees feed on flower nectar, pollen rubs onto their body. When this rubs onto the female parts of another flower, fertilization occurs and new seeds start to form.

Which animals are under threat?

When you look at any type of animal in the world, such as mammals, birds, fish, reptiles, amphibians, and invertebrates, you find species that are under threat and critically endangered in every group. Across the planet, one-eighth of bird species, one-fifth of mammal species, and one-third of amphibian species is endangered.

WHY ARE SOME SPECIES MORE AT RISK?

Some groups or species of animal are more vulnerable than others. For example, large mammals, such as whales, are usually slow to reproduce, so when populations drop in size they are slow to recover. Almost one-third of

Numbers of threatened animal species by major groups

	Number of known species	Proportion of threatened species
Vertebrates		
Amphibians	5,743	31%
Mammals	5,416	20%
Birds	9,917	12%
Reptiles	8,163	4%
Fish	28,500	3%
Invertebrates		
Molluscs	70,000	1%
Crustaceans	40,000	1%
Insects	950,000	0.1%
Others	130,200	0.02%

Source: IUCN Red List of Threatened Species

amphibian species are under threat, in part because frogs and toads have absorbent skins they use to breathe. As they breathe, they also absorb water and any chemicals dissolved in it. Even low levels of pollution can damage their skin so they cannot breathe.

KEYSTONE SPECIES

Together, the animals, plants, and the place they live form a complex community called an **ecosystem.** Organisms in an ecosystem are interdependent – they rely on each other for survival. Some species are so important to an ecosystem that if they become extinct, the whole ecosystem is threatened. These are called **keystone species.** Keystone species can be very small, for example tiny insects that **pollinate** flowers of trees whose fruit is eaten by other species. They can also be large, such as sea otters. Without sea otters, there is a huge increase in the population of sea urchins that the sea otters usually eat. The sea urchins then devour and destroy the kelp (seaweed) forests, which are the main food source for many other marine animals.

Black-tailed prairie dog: A keystone species

The black-tailed prairie dog is a keystone species of the American prairie ecosystem, where over 200 animal species rely on this small, chubby rodent for survival. Black-tailed prairie dogs are a vital source of food for many animals including coyotes, hawks, eagles, badgers, and the endangered black-footed ferret. Their burrows act as homes to other creatures, such as burrowing owls, snakes, and insects. Their burrowing activity loosens soil and their droppings increase the soil's fertility, and many animals graze the healthy plants around their burrows. The extinction of the black-tailed prairie dog would be disastrous for the entire Great Plains ecosystem.

Although black-tailed prairie dogs are listed by IUCN as a lower risk species, ranchers killed many in the past and they are not as common as they once were.

Animals under threat

Habitat destruction is the biggest threat to most animal species – an area of wild land bigger than the whole of North America will probably be destroyed by human activity in the next 30 years. Loss of habitat is the main reason that 80 per cent of endangered mammals are at risk.

CAUSES OF HABITAT LOSS

Human demand for agricultural land has been the main cause of world **deforestation, grassland** clearance, and **wetland** drainage. When people build dams, divert water for **irrigation,** and dredge waterways they change the flow of water and damage rivers and marshes. In the United States, more than half of the original wetlands have been lost in the last 300 years. People also cut down trees and use the timber for building and paper-making. As the world population grows, more and more land is taken over for building cities, roads, airports, and amenities.

EFFECTS OF HABITAT LOSS

There are some obvious effects of habitat loss. Without a place to find food, keep warm, and have young, animals starve, freeze, and fail to reproduce. Larger animals, such as primates, are particularly at risk because they need large areas of habitat to provide the range of food they eat. Less than 2 per cent of the orang-utan's original forest habitat in Borneo and Sumatra remains and orang-utan numbers dropped over 90 per cent in the 20th century.

Other effects of habitat loss are less obvious, but equally damaging. Migrating birds stopover at wetlands and grasslands along their route between winter and summer habitats to rest and feed. Migrant bird populations are now 40 per cent down because their stopover habitats are being destroyed.

In the last 25 years, India's human population has grown by 500 million, and the destruction of the Bengal tiger's habitat has increased accordingly.

Coral reefs

Coral reefs are formed from coral polyps, tiny marine animals that secrete a protective mineral skeleton around themselves. When they die, colonies of coral leave behind a stony structure called a reef. Coral reefs are one of the most diverse habitats in the world, but one in ten reefs have been destroyed, and over half are endangered. Tourists and divers buy or take coral as souvenirs. Fishermen blow up reefs with explosives to kill fish. Coral reefs are also affected by **global warming**. Polyps are sensitive to temperature and many die as oceans get warmer.

These pictures show an unspoilt reef bursting with colour and life, and a coral reef turned to lifeless rubble after being blasted by fishermen.

In Florida, United States, the major cause of death of the endangered Florida panther is being hit by cars as they try to cross the roads that divide their habitat.

Fragmentation

Habitat change can be as damaging to wildlife as habitat destruction. In many parts of the world, habitats have not been entirely destroyed but fragmented – divided up into smaller isolated patches. In forests, loggers have fragmented animal territories and, in rivers, fish habitats have been fragmented by dams and channels. Increasingly, roads cut through grasslands and break these once vast tracts of land into small patches or islands of habitat.

PROBLEMS FOR WILDLIFE

Fragmentation means that groups of animals become trapped in a small area, unable to move because that would mean going through settlements, or over roads where they could be injured. They may be cut off from good food sources or from others of their species to mate with. In times of difficulty, such as **drought**, when watering holes dry up, animals are not able to move to new areas that would have the water they need.

LIFE AT THE EDGE

When habitats are broken up into smaller pieces, animals that once lived in the centre of a habitat may suddenly find themselves living on an edge next to cleared land. Animals living at the edge face many problems. For example, hunters can reach them more easily and they may be more exposed to the stresses of heat, wind, or harsh weather. There is also the risk of increased **predation**. Birds that once nested deep in a forest often find themselves at the boundary of a cleared area where predators can more easily raid their nest and eat their young.

Giant pandas

The giant panda's mountain forest habitat, in southwest China, has been fragmented into about 20 separate patches. Giant pandas eat almost exclusively bamboo. Adults need up to 40 kg (88 lbs) – that's the weight of 160 large carrots – every day! Periodically, bamboo naturally dies back. When this happens in one small area, the pandas are unable to move to new areas with healthy bamboo.

The other result of fragmentation is reduced reproductive rates. Giant pandas live alone and males and females only find each other once a year to mate. If there are towns in the way, they cannot meet up to reproduce, so fewer cubs are born.

Giant panda populations are small and isolated from each other.

Pollution

Pollution happens when poisons or other substances get into and damage the planet's ecosystems. For example, waterways and land are polluted by sewage, industrial waste, and litter, or by agricultural chemicals and oils washed from fields and roads by rain. When **fossil fuels** are burned in power stations, they release poisonous gases that cause air pollution. When oil tankers run aground, their spilled cargo pollutes ocean waters and coasts.

Arctic POPs

Pollution in one area can also affect distant ecosystems. POPs (persistent organic pollutants) are mainly industrial and agricultural chemicals from across the world, which drift by sea or air and accumulate in the Arctic. Under cold Arctic conditions, POPs degrade at an incredibly slow rate and enter **food chains**. For example, contaminated plankton are eaten by fish, which are eaten by seals, which in turn are eaten by polar bears.

As larger mammals eat smaller animals, POPs become concentrated in the fatty tissues that protect them from the cold. On average, there are about ten times more POPs in Arctic mammals, such as seals, than any other animals, even those near the source of the pollution.

This diagram shows the way that POPs move through the Arctic food chain and concentrate in the bodies of the larger animals at the top of the chain.

contaminants

EFFECTS OF POLLUTION

Pollution can affect animals directly, for example, when litter entangles them, suffocates them, or is eaten. Lost nylon fishing nets, rope, and plastic waste kill 2 million seabirds and 100,000 marine mammals every year. Some pollutants in the air combine with water to form **acid rain**, which can kill freshwater fish when it falls in lakes.

Chemical pollution in water and soil passes from plants and small animals through food webs to larger animals. These chemicals can build up within an animal's body and cause reduced reproductive rates, birth defects, deformities, and fatal conditions such as cancer. The chemicals also weaken **immune systems**, making animals more likely to die if they become sick.

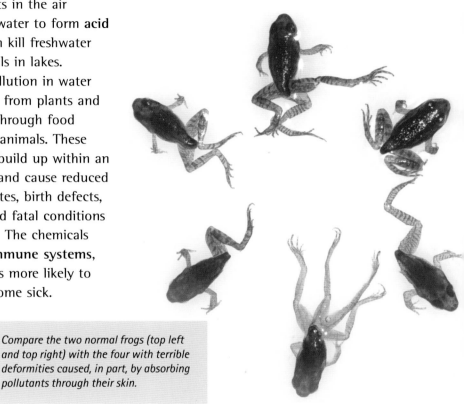

Compare the two normal frogs (top left and top right) with the four with terrible deformities caused, in part, by absorbing pollutants through their skin.

What you can do to reduce pollution

- Reduce air pollution by riding a bicycle or walking, instead of travelling by car.
- Use "environmentally-friendly" cleaning products that do not contribute to water pollution.
- Use your own bags to carry shopping and buy products with less plastic packaging.
- If you spot pollution, such as oil on a beach or in a stream, report it to the local council or Environmental Health Officer.

Wild goats, introduced to the Galapagos Islands by farmers, are stripping grazing habitats vital to the survival of the endangered giant tortoise.

Unwanted arrivals

After habitat loss, the biggest threat to the world's wildlife is the introduction of non-**native** or invader species. When people bring new plants or animals into an area, they often have a destructive impact on the original wildlife there. Alien invaders have caused the extinction of hundreds of animals.

WHY ARE INVADER SPECIES INTRODUCED?

Some invader animal species arrive in a new place accidentally. For example, frogs or spiders can be **imported** in crates of fruit and vegetables. In the past others were brought in by sailors and farmers to provide milk, meat, or fur and some were brought in as pets or for sport. Over time, these animals escaped or were released to live in the wild. In some places, cats were brought in to keep down populations of other **introduced species**, such as rats, that had become a problem. They then become a threat to native species themselves!

WHAT DO YOU THINK?
Culling invader species

In some places, people advocate culling – killing introduced species to try to control them.

- Is it acceptable to kill some animals to protect native species?
- Or is it wrong to kill any wild animals and should more humane methods be found to limit their numbers?

Australia

In Australia, in 1859, 24 rabbits were introduced for food and fur. They bred and spread rapidly and, today, there are over 600 million of them. Rabbits compete with, and displace, native animals and destroy plant life, leaving dry, eroded landscapes. In the 1870s, farmers introduced stoats, weasels, and ferrets in an attempt to kill the rabbits. But these animals also attacked the native species and have since wiped out many of Australia's species of ground-nesting birds.

PROBLEMS WITH UNWANTED ARRIVALS

When a new animal species is introduced, **prey** animals often have no defences against it, so they are easily caught and killed. Because new species often don't have any predators either, there is nothing to keep their numbers down. Other unwanted arrivals harm native animals indirectly by competing with them for food or space, or by introducing new diseases. Sometimes, invader plants destroy wildlife. For example, in the United Kingdom, tree mallow plants have covered land so thickly in places that puffins cannot make their ground nests and there has been a catastrophic decline in puffin breeding.

Non-native red foxes were introduced to California, United States, decades ago for fox hunting and fur farming. They prey on and have severely reduced populations of reptiles, waterbirds, and ground-nesting bird species.

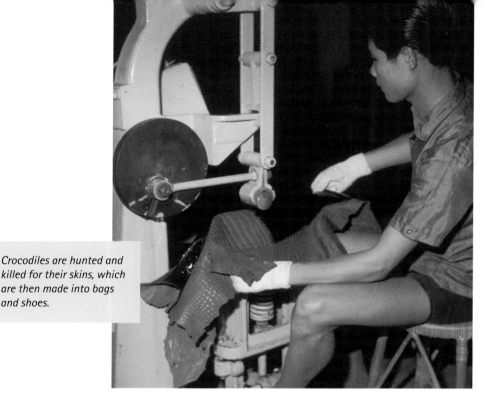

Crocodiles are hunted and killed for their skins, which are then made into bags and shoes.

Hunting and trading

Another way in which the world's animals are under threat is from hunting and trading. Hundreds of millions of animals are traded across country borders each year. In the past, most animals were hunted for food or as trophies to prove a hunter's skill, but today animals are also caught, killed, or sold for other reasons. Many are sold as pets or for zoos or circuses – for example, over 1.5 million live birds are traded every year. Much of the wildlife trade is legal, but hunting and trading are still major threats to species survival.

ANIMALS FOR FOOD

Many animals are trapped or killed for food. Worldwide fisheries have wiped out more than 90 per cent of large fish from the oceans and once-common species, such as Atlantic cod, are drastically reduced. Every two minutes a small whale, dolphin, or porpoise gets entangled in fishing gear and dies, and around 250,000 marine turtles a year suffer the same fate.

In Africa, chimpanzees, gorillas, and other mammals are hunted for their meat, known as "bushmeat". In Tanzania, hunters can earn £13.50 (US$25) for a single chimpanzee carcass, more than most Africans earn in a month.

Pet orang-utans

Poachers shoot around 1,000 adult orang-utans each year so they can take their babies to sell as pets in Asian countries such as Thailand and Taiwan. Four out of every five babies die – due to poor handling, being cramped in boxes on long journeys by ship, or from lack of maternal care. Orang-utans will be at risk until more people learn about the destruction they cause by buying wild animals as pets.

On average, two adults are killed to secure the capture of every one baby orang-utan like this.

ORNAMENTS AND MEDICINES

People carve ornaments from rare turtle shells and elephant tusks. They kill endangered big cats for their fur, alligators and other reptiles for their skin for shoes and handbags, and rhinos so their horns can be made into ceremonial knife handles. Parts of some endangered animals, such as tigers and bears, are used in traditional Chinese medicines. In 1993, more than one million Saiga antelope lived on the grasslands of central Asia, but by 2004 just 30,000 remained – a drop of 97 per cent. Males are killed for their horns, which are used in fever remedies.

What you can do

- When abroad, never buy souvenirs made from wildlife, such as shells, coral, elephant ivory, or rhino horn.
- If you want a parrot as a pet, make sure it has not been taken from the wild.
- Avoid buying and eating fish species that are being overfished.

Finding solutions

Across the planet, conservation groups agree that the best way of saving animals is to protect their natural habitats. Today, there are more than 44,000 **reserves**, national parks, sanctuaries, and other safe havens for wildlife, covering almost 14 million square kilometres (5.4 million square miles). This is an area equivalent in size to India and China combined, or 10 per cent of the planet's land surface.

HOW DO RESERVES WORK?

Reserves cordon off an area of land or sea to protect the plants and animals in it. In many marine reserves, which currently cover only 1 per cent of seas and oceans, fishing is forbidden to allow fish populations to recover. In land reserves, development, tree felling, and agriculture are usually prevented and attempts are made to limit pollution. Some reserves are wilderness areas where people leave the wildlife and plants of an ecosystem to flourish naturally. People manage other nature reserves to ensure the health of the animals there. For example, they might remove **exotic** plants and plant local native species in their place.

Animals such as rhinos have to be sedated in order to move them from areas where they are in danger to the safety of a reserve. This is called translocation.

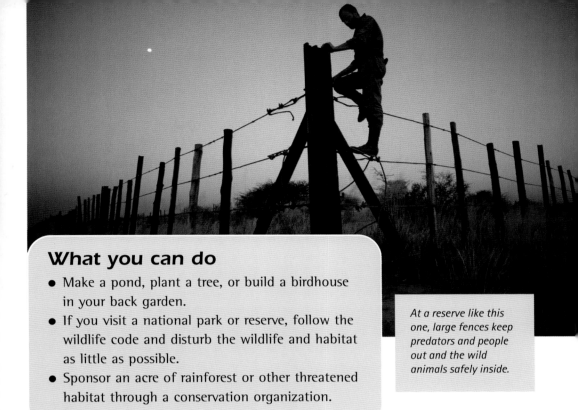

What you can do

- Make a pond, plant a tree, or build a birdhouse in your back garden.
- If you visit a national park or reserve, follow the wildlife code and disturb the wildlife and habitat as little as possible.
- Sponsor an acre of rainforest or other threatened habitat through a conservation organization.

At a reserve like this one, large fences keep predators and people out and the wild animals safely inside.

HABITAT CORRIDORS

For bigger animals, such as elephants, it is important to create large reserves where they can roam widely, but also to plant or maintain forest or grassland corridors so animals can travel between fragmented habitats.

In some areas, such corridors are created by paying farmers to set aside strips of land between reserves. Buffer zones – wide strips of land – between reserves and populated areas are also important, especially as domestic mammals, such as dogs, may roam up to 5 kilometres (3 miles) into a rainforest to eat wild birds and their eggs.

WHAT DO YOU THINK?
Save the rainforests, forget the fields?

- In a world where money for conservation is limited, many people believe it is crucial to identify conservation priorities, such as tropical forests and coral reefs.
- But is it right that these should take priority over other habitats just because they have greater biodiversity?

Legal aid

Various international and national laws and agreements protect animals under threat. Some laws protect ecosystems, such as wetlands or rainforest. Other laws are intended to prevent the trade in animals or animal parts to conserve wild populations. Such laws are an essential part of wildlife conservation. The ban on whaling enforced by the International Whaling Commission from 1986 has saved some species of whale, such as the blue whale, from extinction. International cooperation like this is vital because trade in wild animals crosses borders between countries.

PROBLEMS WITH ENFORCEMENT

The problem with any laws is enforcing them. The rewards are so great that poachers will bribe wardens to hunt animals within protected areas. **Less-developed countries** often do not have the funds to pay for enough wardens or police to enforce laws adequately, so the problems continue. For example, trade in elephant ivory was banned in 1990, but 4,000 elephants are still killed illegally each year. Even when traders are caught, punishments and fines are rarely severe enough to stop them trying it again.

In just five years, between 1999 and 2004, 81 tiger skins and 1,062 leopard skins were seized from criminals involved in this illegal trade in China, India, and Nepal.

CITES

CITES (the Convention on International Trade in Endangered Species of Wild Fauna and Flora) is an international agreement between many governments to ensure that international trade in wild animals and plants does not threaten their survival. It was set up in 1973 and today has about 170 member countries and protects roughly 5,000 different animal species.

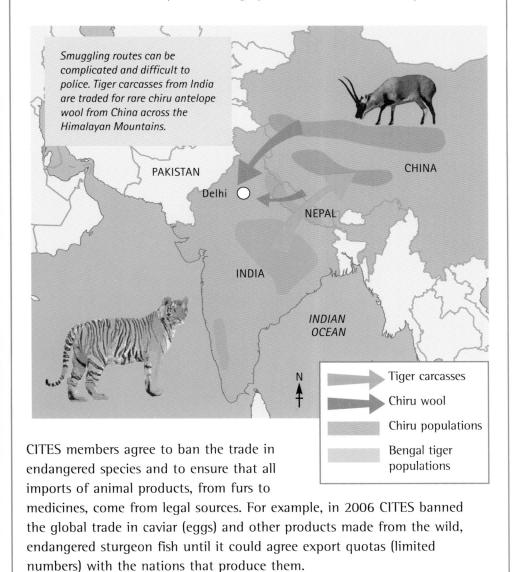

Smuggling routes can be complicated and difficult to police. Tiger carcasses from India are traded for rare chiru antelope wool from China across the Himalayan Mountains.

PAKISTAN

CHINA

Delhi

NEPAL

INDIA

INDIAN OCEAN

N

Tiger carcasses
Chiru wool
Chiru populations
Bengal tiger populations

CITES members agree to ban the trade in endangered species and to ensure that all imports of animal products, from furs to medicines, come from legal sources. For example, in 2006 CITES banned the global trade in caviar (eggs) and other products made from the wild, endangered sturgeon fish until it could agree export quotas (limited numbers) with the nations that produce them.

In a captive breeding centre, orphaned mammals such as this bear cub may be bottle-fed until they are old enough to feed themselves.

Captive breeding

Captive breeding is when wild animals are captured and kept in zoos and other safe havens to breed safely. As the number of their offspring grows, some may be released into suitable habitats to increase or re-establish wild populations.

HOW CAPTIVE BREEDING WORKS

Each individual has a unique group or pool of **genes**, but closely related individuals have similar gene pools. Inbreeding is when closely related individuals mate. Their offspring inherit similar gene pools from their parents and these are less likely to contain the different genes that may help them thrive. Inbred animals are sometimes weak, prone to illness, and less able to survive the stresses of the habitat they live in than offspring from unrelated parents.

Captive animals generally live in small populations and are more likely to inbreed. Captive breeding centres share records of the relatedness of captive individuals of different species. They make sure animals that mate are as unrelated as possible to ensure the genetic health of the entire captive population.

PROBLEMS

Captive breeding has a low success rate. Only one in ten captive mammal species breed successfully. Many species, such as giant pandas, only breed if there is minimal human contact, which is tricky in places where paying visitors help fund breeding programmes.

It is difficult to reintroduce captive-bred animals into the wild. Many die because they cannot fend for themselves. For example, tiger cubs learn to hunt from their mothers in the wild, but in zoos people feed tigers. In some cases, captive-bred animals cannot be reintroduced into the wild because there is little suitable habitat left. However, captive breeding is an important conservation tool and conservationists estimate that 2,000 species may only escape extinction through captive breeding programmes.

The Californian condor

In 1987, the Californian condor, the largest flying bird in North America, was nearly extinct. Its total wild population had fallen to about 20 as a result of hunting and accidental lead poisoning, which was caused by the birds scavenging carcasses that had been killed by hunters and contained shotgun pellets.

All the remaining birds were caught and captive bred at Los Angeles Zoo and the San Diego Wild Animal Park. By 2005, there were about 100 Californian condors living in captivity and almost the same number had been reintroduced into the wild.

The Californian condor is one of the great success stories for captive breeding programmes.

Worldwide, around nine million people go on whale-watching trips every year.

Paying their way

Some conservation works by using animals to make money to pay for their own protection, for example by tourism. Unmanaged tourism can have a negative impact on habitats and wildlife, such as when travellers stray from paths and trample plants, erode land, or scare birds from their nests. Responsible tourism, however, can help to save some of the world's most endangered species. When people visit reserves this increases their understanding of and concern for wild animals, which may persuade governments to offer animals more protection in the future.

TOURISM AND CONSERVATION

When tourists visit national parks and other conservation areas, the money they pay can be used to maintain or improve these reserves. For example, income generated by tourism in Kruger National Park, South Africa, covers all the costs of managing and maintaining the park and pays the wages of the people who work there. In this way, tourism gives habitats an economic value so they are less likely to be developed. Some tour companies that bring visitors to wild areas donate a percentage of their profits to conservation projects. Some people take "volunteer conservation holidays" where they actually work to mend fences or plant trees, as well as generating income for conservation projects.

LEGAL HUNTING

Some countries also use trophy hunting as a wildlife conservation and management tool, especially in areas too remote for most tourists. Hunters are willing to pay large fees to kill some "game" animals. This brings in money to help maintain the reserves.

In some places, governments and conservationists explain to local people the importance of conserving wildlife for the future. They work with villagers to set quotas (limits) on the number of animals that they hunt for food or to sell, and on the size of the area that they hunt in. In areas where local poaching has become a problem, regulating hunting like this can save more animals than trying to outlaw it completely.

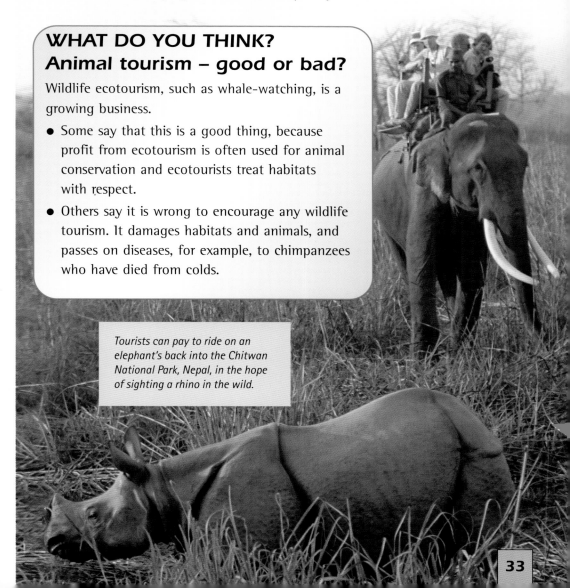

WHAT DO YOU THINK?
Animal tourism – good or bad?

Wildlife ecotourism, such as whale-watching, is a growing business.

- Some say that this is a good thing, because profit from ecotourism is often used for animal conservation and ecotourists treat habitats with respect.

- Others say it is wrong to encourage any wildlife tourism. It damages habitats and animals, and passes on diseases, for example, to chimpanzees who have died from colds.

Tourists can pay to ride on an elephant's back into the Chitwan National Park, Nepal, in the hope of sighting a rhino in the wild.

33

Debates about animals under threat

Many of the world's species-rich areas are located in the **tropics** and less-developed countries, where many people are poor and live in rural areas. Some people say that when relatively rich conservationists from **more-developed countries** call for the conservation of animals and their habitats, poor people lose out. Others argue that, when done properly, both people and animals can reap the benefits of conservation.

PUTTING ANIMALS FIRST

Some people argue that when areas of land are reserved for animals, local people suffer. In Africa, over 100,000 nomadic Maasai people were forced off the land that had always been their home – many into lives of poverty and hunger – to make way for conservation areas such as the Serengeti National Park in Tanzania. They say conservationists have no right to tell people to stop cutting down trees in a reserve, just to save animals like tigers, which cause them nothing but trouble. The local people need the timber for firewood, to cook food in order to survive.

In some parts of Europe, wolf populations are increasing after the success of conservation efforts, but farmers and hunters say they should have the right to kill wolves that attack their livestock.

Ecotourists view the rainforest from a treetop walkway. The money they pay means local people can afford to buy fuel instead of cutting down trees for firewood.

Some also argue that Western compassion for animals, such as lions and elephants, is based on cute cartoon images of them, not the real thing. People in Africa and Asia might have to kill a lion to save their children, or shoot an elephant to stop it trampling their field of crops, in the same way that others kill pests such as locusts and black rats.

LOCALS AND CONSERVATION

Others argue that most conservation projects today do involve or benefit local people. Morally, this is the right thing to do, but it also gives local people a stake in the conservation process and encourages them to save more animals. For example, in a national park or lodge that encourages tourists, up to 2,000 local people can earn a living as guides, drivers, or hotel workers. In some cases, a percentage of the income generated is donated to local community projects, such as building schools.

Tourism also gives people who share a habitat with threatened species a reason to protect the ecosystems. For example, on Mindanao Island in the Philippines, illegal logging by locals has fallen by 95 per cent since 1997 when a rainforest treetop walkway was built to encourage tourists.

Many zoos keep their animals in spacious, comfortable enclosures, but others, such as this one in Vietnam, imprison animals in appalling conditions.

Are zoos a bad thing?

Millions of animals are kept in captivity and displayed in zoos across the world and more than 600 million people visit zoos each year. That is nearly one-tenth of the total world population. But do all these visits help or hinder threatened animals?

WHAT'S THE PROBLEM WITH ZOOS?

Some people argue that zoos have got a big problem. They are primarily tourist attractions that are out to make money – and the animals that attract visitors are not necessarily the ones that need urgent conservation. Most zoos claim that their breeding programmes and other work are actively helping conservation of endangered species. Yet, nine out of every ten species kept in UK zoos are not threatened – in fact, a quarter of these zoos keep no threatened species at all. Surely zoos should be full of the rarest animals around?

Many people argue that, instead of captive breeding programmes in zoos, all conservation efforts should be focused on habitat conservation or creating forest corridors to solve fragmentation problems. Otherwise, there won't be any habitats left to release the animals into anyway.

ON THE OTHER HAND...

Advocates (supporters) of zoos say that zoos help populations of endangered animals in many ways. They help to raise awareness of problems, such as habitat destruction, pollution, and poaching, by using information displays near animal cages and education programmes. They encourage donations to help conservation of wild animals in various ways. These include maintaining wildlife reserves and employing scientists to study animals in order to identify conservation priorities. Their captive breeding programmes can raise numbers of threatened species. Although reintroduction into the wild is not always possible, zoos help maintain a genetic bank of rare creatures that may be able to live wild in the future, once suitable habitats become available. So, what do you think? Are zoos good or bad?

Black lion tamarin

Black lion tamarins are tiny monkeys with mane-like hair around their faces. They are very rare in their native country, Brazil, due to habitat destruction. They breed well in captivity but reintroduction is difficult because zoo-bred animals lack survival skills. For example, some reintroduced tamarins were picked off easily by predators and could not find enough food. Durrell Wildlife Conservation Trust on the island of Jersey, UK, is now training its captive-bred tamarins to search more effectively for food – for example, by adding rope-ways to enclosures to encourage them to explore and forage for food.

The black lion tamarin is one of the world's most endangered mammal species.

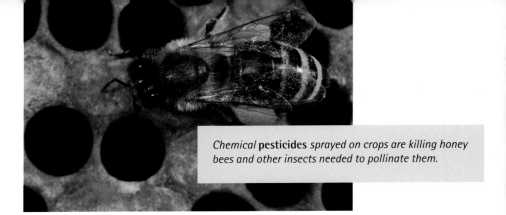

Chemical **pesticides** *sprayed on crops are killing honey bees and other insects needed to pollinate them.*

Does biodiversity matter?

Biodiversity is the total of all living species in an ecosystem. In natural ecosystems unchanged by people, the biodiversity has developed over millions of years through evolution. There is an interconnected web of plants and animals. For example, many plants need bees to pollinate their flowers so they can reproduce. The animals that eat the plants, such as caterpillars and rabbits, are themselves vital food sources for other animals, such as birds and foxes.

SELF-REGULATING EARTH

Some people ask why we should care about biodiversity. In the past, when animals have become extinct, other species have taken the place of those that disappeared and biodiversity has naturally changed. After all, natural selection means that some species thrive in changed circumstances – for example, raccoons are flourishing in Florida habitats that have been fragmented by spreading settlements. People also put forward the case that it is silly to preserve every species, regardless of what it is. There are some animals that most people agree we would be better off without, such as the tiny blood parasites that cause malaria or crop-destroying locusts.

STEWARDSHIP

Others argue that it is important to act as stewards and protect Earth's biodiversity, because of the vital resources it provides, such as medicine and food. Almost one-quarter of all modern prescription drugs, including aspirin, are derived from plant sources. When we chop down rainforests or destroy coral reefs, we may also be ruining our chances of finding cures to diseases. One-sixth of people on Earth get more than one-third of their total protein from ocean fish. Destroying reefs to develop beach resorts takes away one of the main places where young tropical fish live.

Cone shells

Many tourists to tropical beaches think cone shells are pretty souvenirs. However, millions of these shells are killed each year for sale and their reef and mangrove habitats destroyed. Scientists have discovered that the 600 species of cone shells produce thousands of different poisons that they use to kill their prey. These poisons could be used to treat anything from cancer to arthritis; one provides pain relief a thousand times more effective than morphine. Scientists are calling for tropical nations to protect reefs and control the shell trade to preserve this potentially life-saving biodiversity.

Could tropical cone shells like these provide cures for fatal human conditions, such as cancer and heart irregularities?

The future

Over the next 30 years, up to one-quarter of all known mammals and one-tenth of all recorded bird species could die out. Many people fear that threats to animals and their habitats will only increase in the future because of global warming, which will bring more extreme weather and threaten more habitats.

GLOBAL WARMING

Many scientists predict that in the future climate change will endanger one-quarter of the species on Earth. For example, one result of global warming is melting ice caps at the North and South Poles. The ice is breaking up earlier in the year than it used to 50 years ago, which means that polar bears are unable to catch and eat enough seals from ledges of sea ice. They then cannot store enough fat to survive hibernation once the Arctic winter sets in. Melting ice caps also increase global sea levels. As some coastal areas are submerged, sea turtles, which bury their eggs in sand, will lose many nesting sites.

Some scientists fear that the polar bear could be extinct within 100 years, in part as a result of global warming.

Looking to the future

The Convention on Biological Diversity is an agreement between world governments to significantly reduce the loss of biodiversity by 2010, for example, by using the planet's natural resources more sustainably. As part of this project, the United Nations proclaimed 22 May "The International Day for Biological Diversity" to increase public awareness of the problem. On this day each year, wildlife sanctuaries offer free visits or guided tours to encourage people to understand and care about these ecosystems. For example, in Scotland in 2004, activities to mark the day included moth walks, talks and exhibitions, bird-box making, and animal tracking.

HOPE FOR THE FUTURE

Conservation solutions are already underway – from taking steps to control invasive alien species in ecosystems to reducing the number of grassland and savannah habitats that are being changed to farmland and urban settlements. Scientists are always looking for new solutions. For example, seeds obtained from the droppings of the cat-like mammals called civet cats have been found to grow into healthy rainforest trees because they are enriched by chemicals in the cats' stomachs. Now they are being planted at the edge of coffee plantations in the hills of Anamalai in south India, to expand areas of rainforest for wildlife in the region, such as elephants and leopards. Further study of animals and habitats will produce other innovative conservation solutions. Together, many small conservation projects will make a big difference and give hope for future biodiversity.

Dodo birds once roamed the tropical island of Mauritius, but became extinct when humans over-hunted them in the 17th century. They can now only be seen in museums. Is this the way we want to see orang-utans and tigers in the future?

41

Statistical information

Protected land

The extent of land protected as, for example, nature reserves or wilderness areas, varies greatly across the world, as these figures show.

Protected area as percentage of total land area, 2005

Bhutan	29.6
Germany	29.3
Denmark	21.8
Israel	18.4
UK	15.3
Russian Federation	5.4
India	4.9
Egypt	4.6
France	3.0
Ireland	1.1
Bangladesh	0.5
Bosnia and Herzegovina	0.5

Source: Earth Trends, Protected Areas, 2005

Nature reserves

Here are the numbers of nature reserves, wilderness areas, and national parks in different continents in 2005.

Oceania	2,693
North America	2,666
Europe	2,329
Asia	729
South America	557
Central/Southern Africa	299
Central America/Caribbean	214
Middle East/North Africa	81
Total world	**9,568**

Source: IUCN

Tropical forest

Tropical forest biomes cover around 6 per cent of all land, yet provide homes for over 50 per cent of the world's species. How much of the tropical forest is being protected in each continent containing this biome?

Asia	16.4%
South America	12.2%
Central America/Caribbean	12.0%
Africa	9.1%
Oceania	9.1%

Source: WWF

Madagascan animals under threat

Extensive deforestation and a population rising by 3 per cent each year is putting pressure on Madagascar's endemic animals. Here is the number of threatened animal species in 2000.

Mammals	50
Invertebrates	30
Birds	27
Reptiles	18
Fish	13
Amphibians	2

Source: www.redlist.org

Tiger population

Wild tigers are disappearing because of hunting in the past and poaching today.

1900	100,000
1950	60,000
1960	45,000
1970	30,000
1980	25,000
1990	7,000
2000	2,000
2025	?

Source: Earthscan Atlas of Endangered Species

Legal trade in live parrots

Look how many live parrots were traded in 2002 by CITES members from different continents.

These continents import more than they export

Europe	137,082
Asia	43,634
Middle East/North Africa	40,945
North America	36,241

These continents export more than they import

Central/Southern Africa	198,174
South America	46,218
Oceania	11,136
Central America/Caribbean	2,370

Source: Earth Trends, Protected Areas, 2005

Glossary

acid rain rain that has become acidic by contact with air pollution

adapted when an animal has inherited certain characteristics that enable it to live in one type of climate or another

biodiversity number and variety of plants, animals, and other organisms in a particular place

biome large ecosystem that is defined by its climate and the unique plants and animals that live there

climate usual weather a region experiences at a particular time of year

climate change major change in the long-term climate of an area or of the world. Climate change in the past had natural causes – ice ages were caused by changes in the distance between Earth and the Sun.

conservation protecting and preserving plant and animal species and their habitats

coral reef rock-like structures built by small ocean animals called polyps

deforestation destruction of forests

drought when an area suffers a long period of time without rain or with too little rain

ecosystem system made up of all the animals and plants in a community (in an area)

endemic plant and animal species living only in a certain limited area and nowhere else

evolution process by which all plant and animal species change gradually over time because of slight variations in the genes that one generation passes to the next

exotic plants not native to a place

extinct no longer in existence

flagship species species that are popular and appealing and attract public support for their conservation

food chain group of animals and plants in which each member eats or is eaten by the next member of the "chain"

fossil fuels fuels, such as oil, natural gas, and coal, formed in the ground over millions of years from remains of dead plants and animals

genes chemical units offspring inherit from their parents, which determine specific characteristics, such as eye colour

global warming rise in temperatures across the world, caused by polluting gases in the air

grassland biome in which grasses are the major plant species, such as Asian steppe, American prairie, and African savannah

habitat natural home of a group of plants or animals. A river is one kind of habitat.

immune system animal's body system of defences against disease and infections

imported goods brought into a country from a foreign source

introduced species plant or animal species that was brought by humans into an area where it previously did not exist

irrigation supplying water for crops, parks, golf courses, and lawns

keystone species species with a key role in an ecosystem, whose removal leads to other extinctions within that ecosystem

less-developed countries poorer, less-industrialized nations of the world, such as India

more-developed countries wealthiest, most industrialized nations of the world, such as those of Western Europe and the United States

native species that originated naturally in a particular region

pesticides chemicals used to kill pests and limit the damage they do to crops

poachers people who illegally hunt or fish

pollinate transfer pollen from the flower of one plant to another of the same species, allowing the plant to grow fruits and seeds so new plants can grow

pollution when part of the natural world is contaminated by harmful substances as a result of human activities

predation when animals catch and eat other animals

prey animals that are eaten by other animals

reserve area of land set aside and managed for conservation

species group of animals that can breed together and does not usually breed with other species

species diversity number of different species in a given area

tropics area of Earth either side of the Equator, between the Tropic of Cancer and the Tropic of Capricorn

tundra frozen, treeless plain found near polar ice

wetlands swamps and other damp areas of land

Further information

Books

The *Animals Under Threat* series (Heinemann Library, 2004–2005) highlights the plight of animals that are endangered or threatened by extinction. There are separate books on *Black Asian Elephant, Black Rhino, Killer Whale, Bengal Tiger, Alligator, Great White Shark, Mountain Gorilla, Giant Panda, Orang-utan, Koala, Grey Wolf,* and *Peregrine Falcon.* The human involvement in the threat to these animals or their habitat is discussed, and the conservation efforts being made to avoid extinction are detailed.

Myers, Norman (editor). *The Gaia Atlas of Planet Management* (Gaia Books, 2000)
This atlas has information on a wide range of issues that affect the well-being of Earth and how people can establish a sustainable future for themselves and the planet.

Few, Roger. *Plant Action: Animal Watch* (Dorling Kindersley, 2001)
This book explains current concerns about the world's habitats and wildlife and helps plan the future with practical ideas that can really make a difference.

Kendall, Patricia. *Worldwatch: WWF* (Hodder Children's Books, 2003)
This provides an insight into the aims and methods of this world-famous conservation and environmental organization and discusses the complex problems it is trying to address.

Websites

You can explore the Internet to find out more about animals under threat. Websites can change, so if the links below no longer work use a reliable search engine.

WWF
www.panda.org
At the web home of the conservation organization WWF there are homework help sections, fact sheets about endangered animals and habitats, and a wealth of information about conservation projects and how they work.

Goodzoos.com
www.goodzoos.com/conserva.htm
Find out more about where the good zoos are in the world and what criteria zoo inspectors use to judge them.

ARKive
www.arkive.org
ARKive has a vast library of films, photographs, and audio recordings of life on Earth that you can look at and download for projects or personal use. It also has fascinating information and facts about world habitats, plants, and animals.

Conservation International
www.biodiversityhotspots.org/xp/Hotspots
Information about the richest and most threatened reservoirs of animal life on Earth.

United Nations Environment Programme
http://bure.unep-wcmc.org/imaps/gb2002/book/viewer.htm
On this UNEP website you can access some interesting maps showing biodiversity today, and how it has changed over time.

Contact addresses

WWF International
Avenue du Mont Blanc
1196 Gland
Switzerland

Greenpeace International
Ottho Heldringstraat 5
1066 AZ Amsterdam
The Netherlands

IUCN
Rue Mauverny
28 Gland
Switzerland

Friends of the Earth International
PO Box 19199, 1000 GD Amsterdam
The Netherlands

INDEX

Titles in the *Planet Under Pressure* series include:

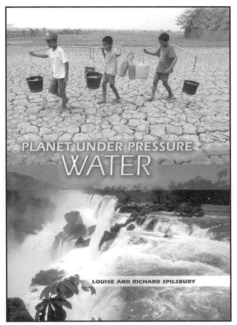

Hardback   1 4062 0534 6

Hardback   1 4062 0535 4

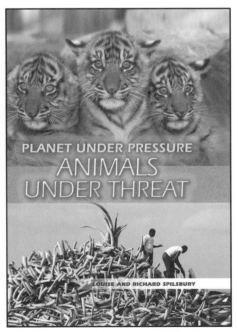

Hardback   1 4062 0537 0

Hardback   1 4062 0536 2

Find out about other titles from Heinemann Library on our website www.heinemann.co.uk/library